D1034736

# A WALK WITH ME

Gwen Frostic

. . . . if a little toad winks

as you pass by - - - -

or you wish he would . . . . . . . . .

then this little book is dedicated

to you . . . . . . . . .

Let's just wander here and there - - - -
like leaves floating in the autumn air
and look at common little things - - - - -
stones on the beach - - -
flowers turning into berries . . . . . .

. . . . from the winds we'll catch a bit
of that wondrous feeling that comes - - -
- - not from seeing - - - -
but from being part of nature . . . . .

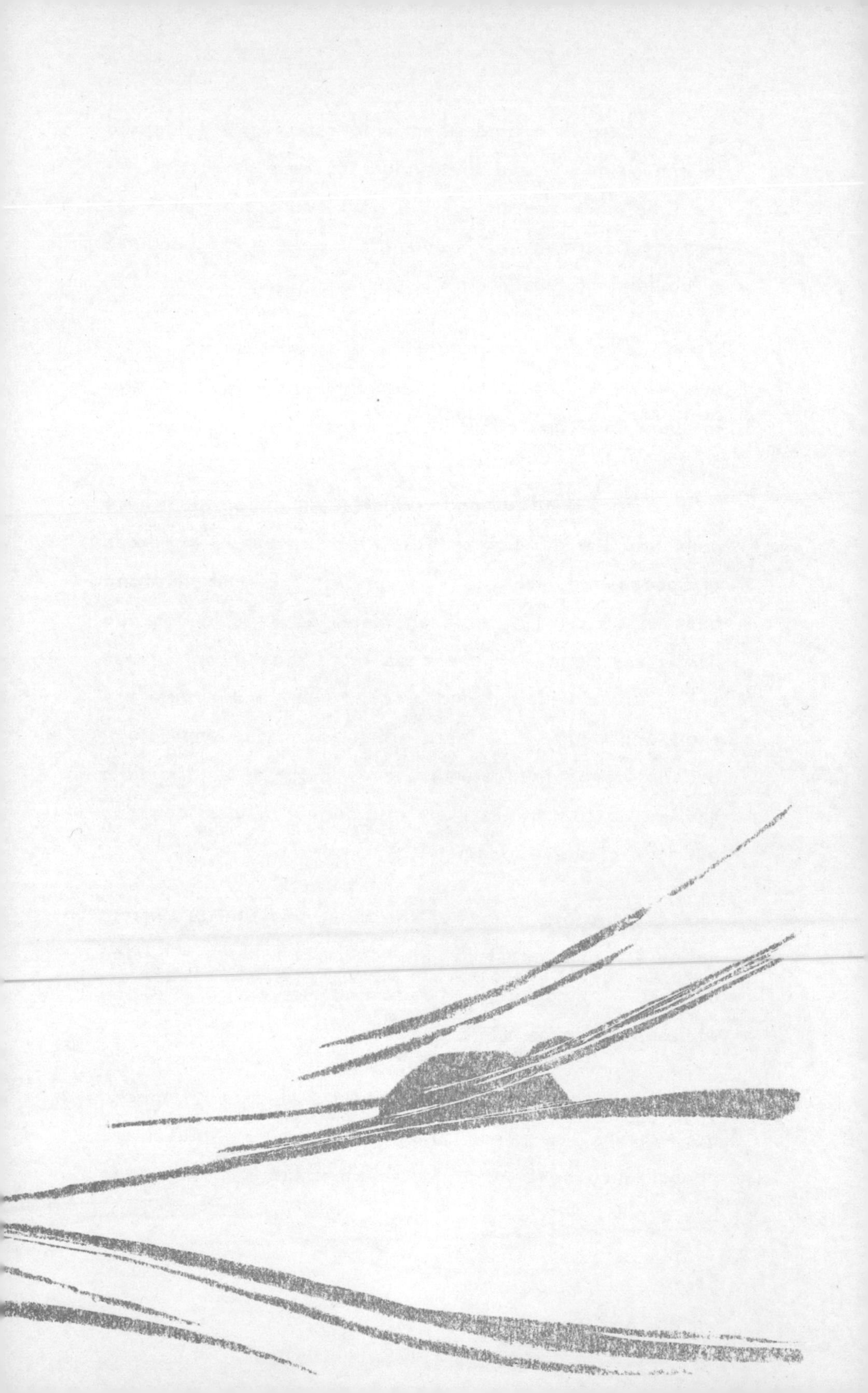

There is a time when wild asters and goldenrod fill the fields - - and the sumac leaves turn scarlet - - - - a time when the air - - the light and the moisture are in perfect harmony - - - and the whole world becomes a fairyland of mushrooms . . . . . . . . . . .

As if by magic they push their way up - - - - everywhere - - no stone - - no log can stop them now for their time has come . . . . . . . . . . .

What great fun and creative imagination must have gone into the molding of these little things - - - hundreds of shapes and sizes - - - - - just as many shades and hues . . . . . . Tiny dots on stems so delicate you can hardly see them - - huge ones more than a foot across - - - some beautiful and graceful - - - some round - - short and pudgy - - there are those whose caps sit at odd angles on their stems - - - those that form little shelves on tree trunks - - - and perfect rosettes covering old logs of the woods . . . . . . . .

Here are some of the most beautiful browns in nature - - - the most delicate pinks and blues - - - the deepest - - most startling reds and yellows - - - and whites as pure as white can be . . . . . . . .

- - - and so they grow on old stumps - - among dead leaves - - - on fallen trees - - - - - that these things which have lived may return to the earth - - - - to live again . . . . . . . . . .

There is something mysteriously
beautiful about a dead tree

- - - as it stands no longer resisting
the winds that strip its bark
and twist its trunk . . . . .

In sunshine - rain - - or snow - - -
it seems to suggest a power
long after life has gone . . . . . . .

As the leaves finish their pageant of color and drop to the ground the trees stand in majestic beauty against a clear blue sky and disclose the secrets of the birds held so well all through the summer . . . . . . . .

Masterpieces of artistic construction - - - these homes of the birds . . . Some hanging on the tip ends of branches woven with such craftsmanship that they withstand the strongest winds that blow - - - - - yet sway with the most gentle breeze . . . . Some are beautiful homes with fine strips of birch bark woven into the grasses with caterpillar's silk . . . Some welded to the forks of trees with mud foundations - - - - - - mud carried a bit at a time by the builder making hundreds of trips . . . . . . . . .

There are nests in low bushes and among the reeds of the swamplands - - - - nests used year after year by adding a few more twigs - - a few more grasses . . . . . There are delicate nests - - smaller than a sycamore ball - - covered with tiny lichens - - - saddled to a branch with spider's silk - - - - - yet strong enough to hold two tiny birds in a bed of down . . . . . . . . . . .

Each bird has its own secret of nest building - - - but no bird has more than a bill to weave with - - - a foot to shape with - - - and its own body with which to mold the clay - - - - and so with grasses - roots - twigs - bark - strings - and mud they build their homes in which to raise their young - - - and line them with thistledown - furs - mosses and feathers for comfort . . . . . . . . .

. . . . . and there they are - - - just empty nests - - - - - - - - and yet - - - what marvels they reveal . . . . . . . .

Up on the edge of the bluffs - - -
look far out over the waves
Out where the sky begins - -
and white clouds form
Soon a gull drifts by in the wind - - and little
sandpipers appear on the beach below . . . .

. . . . . . . . . . and you are not alone

In the open fields - - -
where sweet clover blows - - -
and Queen Anne's lace and asters grow
A bumble bee hums among the flowers - - -
and little goldfinches fill the air . . . . .

. . . . . . . . and you are not alone

In the deep woods - -
all seems so still . .
Leaves rustle a bit - and a chipmunk runs - - -
a little toad sits
on the deep green moss . . . .
. . . . . . . . . . and you are not alone

It's times like these
that you come to know -
How much a part of everything you are - - - -
- - - how much all things
are part of you . . . . . . .

A quiet grey sky - - -

- - a few white crystals float in the cool air . . Soon a multitude of snowflakes will be falling - - - the winds will carry them into long beautiful drifts - - and all things will be covered with a white softness . . . . .

On the beach the winds will blow wave upon wave and they will turn into ice - creating fantastic piles and ridges along the water's edge . . . A setting sun will turn the spray of other waves dashing high against the ice into gold and far above the gulls will reflect the golden rays in their feathers . . . . .

With the dawn the sun will reveal a wonderland - - - casting shadows of each twig - - each drift far across the whiteness . . . . . . . The reds of osiers - - the deep greens of pines - - the browns - greys and blacks of tree trunks half covered with snow - - bits of gleaming yellow inside milkweed pods - - - and maroon sumac heads will accent the immaculate earth with color . . . .

At night the full moon will be reflected by thousand upon thousands of tiny crystals - - - - - and - - - everywhere there will be beauty - - mystery - - - stillness - - - simplicity - - - - - and - - - life . . . . . . . .

Gulls . . . .

- - - - - just gulls - - - graceful forever - - -
standing like little ritualistic statues - - -
each facing whatever gale may blow . . .

Gulls . . . .

- - - suddenly filling the air with thousands
of wild wings . . . . . . . . .

Gulls . . . . .

- - - riding the ice that floats and
disappears in the waves of spring . . . .

Gulls . . . .

- - - playmates of the winds - - - calling - -
laughing - - - gliding with effortless beauty
- - - - always with a deep sense of
tranquility . . . . . . . .

Down on the beach the waves leave their marks in the sands - - - sometimes the long sweeping marks of high forceful waves - - - sometimes little scallops made by quiet ripples washing gently on the shore . . . . . . Sandpipers - ducks - - gulls - - - the deer and raccoons come and leave their tracks in the soft sand - - - and the winds leave theirs among the grasses . . . . Marks that tell stories of the day and night - - - but the stones along the water's edge tell stories of thousands of years gone by . . . . . . . . .

Red stones and blue - - greens - browns - yellows and greys - - in combinations that defy description . . . Stones that have traveled far to be here - - - - stones that have many miles to travel ahead . . . Stones that hold true records of prehistoric times . . . Striped stones that reveal the layers of minerals which formed the rock from which they were chipped by the wind - the waters -

the heat and the frost . . . . .

Now and then there is one with ripples on its surface - - - - - - - - - - or raindrop prints made at its hour of formation - - - and bits of coral that developed in warm salt water three hundred thousand years ago . . . . . .

Stones - - - - tumbled by the winds - - - rubbed by the sands - - - washed by the waters - - - ever so slowly turning into sand . . . And the winds - the sands and the waters sculpture some into beautiful forms - - - - and working together etch wondrous designs on others . .

- - - - - and the years go by - - - - as each stone travels ever toward the sea - - - - - it may move with extreme slowness - or rest for ages in the field or lake it matters not - - - for nature has ample time on which to draw - - - but always - - - that which it has created must return - - - to be created anew - - - -
. . . . . . . . for that is the law of the universe . . . .

Birds always sing in the springtime - - -
wind ever blows through the trees - - -
and the sun shall rise each dawn - - -
yet - - this day is a new creation
in the pattern of constant change . . . .

A fresh bed of moss carpets the woods - - as other moss has grown before . . . . The trout lily rises from the earth and blossoms - - - a new - - and an ancient flower . . . . . The beech stump is just a bit farther on its return to the earth as the leaves of new trees are sprouting . . . Birds come and build their nests - - that birds shall always sing and fly . . . . . .

The squirrels jump from limb to limb high in the trees that are ever the same - - - and - - - never the same - - - - - for each day - - - each hour - - - - all things change - - - - - - the trees - - - the flowers - - - rocks - - - - the sand and the waters - - - the birds and all the animals of earth - - - -

- - - yet - life goes on unchanged - - - - - - -
. . . nothing is new
. . . . . . . . nothing is old
this is life . . . . . . . .
and this is eternity . . . . . . .

The exquisite winged nuts of the birch sail in the autumn air - - - - acorns roll along the hillside - - - - the twin seeds of the maples whirl in the early summer sunshine - - - - and willow seeds - covered with long silky down - ride the streams - - - - - the winds catch the delicate seeds of the pines as the cones open and set their wings free . . . . .

. . . the migration of the trees is taking place . . .

Seeds in every conceivable shape - size and color - each with its own means of protection - - each - - its own way of travel - - - each - - a tiny tree within itself . .

Some travel to far-away places - - - some stay close by - - - but soon all come to rest - - - and the snows come - the ice and the winds - - - - - while in the earth life is developing - - - always . . . . . . . . . .

When spring breezes blow warm sunshine over the land - the plant is ready to break out of its tiny world - - to send roots into the earth - - - a stem toward the sky - - - - and a new tree is growing . . . . . . . .

. . . . a tree that in many years to come will stand upright in majestic individuality - - - - - - - - - and bring inspiration to all who see - - - - - -

. . . as long as there are trees in tiny seeds - - -
there will be miracles on earth . . . . .

Follow the path of a stone - - -
that rolls along the beach
Follow the flight of an eagle - - - - -
as he soars in the sky above

Follow the trail of the wind - - - - -
that blows through the top of the trees

Follow the song of a thrush - - - - -
when evening comes to earth
Follow God's moon in the heavens - - -
till it sinks below the lake

. . . and your heart will be filled with wonder - - - - -
and your years will be ever inspired . . . .

Activity . . . intense meaningful activity - - - - - -
prismatic dragonflies darting back and forth - - - flycatchers
- - redwings - - and kingfishers - - blue herons - - -
- - white swan - - geese and eagles - - - - - -
ducks kicking the water as they rise - -
sandpipers - - hawks - - and loons - - -
majestic wings filling the air - - -
wild - - wild calls everywhere . . . . . . . .

And there is calm - - - deep still serenity . . .
Jewelweed glistens in the sunshine - - - cattails sway in
the breeze - - - osier - - milkweed - - trees - - - - each
with its own hour of creation - - each its hour of glory
- - - - and each a final hour when it gives way to that
which is created . . . . There is calmness in the clouds
- - and in a setting sun reflected in quiet waters - - - -
a calmness that is felt . . rather than understood . . . .

One by one the stars come out - - and the creatures
of the night begin to stir - - owls - raccoons - opossums
- - - the spiders that work all night spinning webs that
will be jeweled with morning dew . . . . . . . .

This is the swampland . . . the in-between land . . .
restless . . . . . and serene . . . . .
with rhythmical beauty . . . . . .
always . . . . . . . . . . . . . . .

- - - and so - - - - there has ever been

beauty in a feather
drifting in the wind
beauty in the lichens
growing on a rock
beauty in the star dust
shining in the sun
beauty in the grasses
blowing in a breeze . . . .

- - - - - so - - - - there will ever be - - - - -

wondrous - - - simple - - - beauty
always here on earth . . . . . . . . . . . .